The Hon. Dean Brown AO, former premier of South Australia

"From a childhood in the mountains of Yunnan, China, to flying the Pacific in corporate jets, Ed Yang has experienced different cultures at all levels. This book provides a unique insight into how to respect and understand cultural differences. There is no better teacher than Ed Yang."

****

Jeff Heller, former vice chairman and president of EDS Corporation

"Ed Yang's masterfully simplified words and illustrations reveal the values, customs, and beliefs that are core to shaping the thoughts and actions of the Chinese. This is a must-read primer for anyone desiring to build genuine relationships in China."

****

Matthew Miau, chairman of Mitac-Synnex Corporation

"This book is simple to understand, easy to read, and is perfectly timed for those who are interested in learning the culture of the world's two largest economies. Those who spend effort on gaining such knowledge will be greatly rewarded!"

****

Otis W. Baskin, PhD, emeritus professor of management and former dean, George L. Graziadio School of Business and Management, Pepperdine University

"An insightful and culturally sensitive book, as is to be expected from three individuals with deep experience in both Asian and

Western business society. But beyond the expected, a reader will find practical advice without 'preaching' about American insensitivity. This is an impactful but easy-reading book that will help anyone doing business in China or receiving guests from China to communicate beyond language barriers. The lessons of this book can be absorbed on a flight from Los Angeles to Beijing, but the learning can continue for a career as the advice is applied and understood at continuingly deeper levels. A must-read for anyone doing business in this new age of East–West relations."

****

Kailiang Wu, Amazon fulfillment analytics engineer, MIT alum

"Ed's book will take you through a highly illustrative and thoughtful culture show. As a Chinese professional living in the US, I find the book particularly helpful in realizing my ingrained cultural roots and learning to leverage it in the Western society effectively, knowing the nuance between the two distinct cultures."

****

Jianmin Wu, MBA student at Hult International Business School

"When East meets the West, turning cultural differences into cultural synergy can enlighten and empower. Ed Yang's book takes us on a historical journey by explaining cultural differences in a simple way, and with it, he gives the reader the keys to understanding the intersection of Asian and Western cultures.

"As an international MBA student studying in the USA, I often experience cultural barriers in my daily life. This book has helped me to avoid a feeling of panic and, instead, to be more proactive, more outgoing, and more involved—providing me with a metaphorical hammer to break that crystal glass ceiling."

Confucius Says ...

There Are No Fortune Cookies in China

How Understanding Chinese Culture Is Key to Building Relationships

Edward V. Yang

with **Kate Ou**
and
Dennis Smith

iUniverse LLC
Bloomington

Confucius Says ... There Are No Fortune Cookies in China
How Understanding Chinese Culture Is Key to Building Relationships

iUniverse books may be ordered through booksellers or by contacting:

iUniverse
1663 Liberty Drive
Bloomington, IN 47403
www.iuniverse.com
1-800-Authors (1-800-288-4677)

ISBN: 978-1-4917-0679-4 (sc)
ISBN: 978-1-4917-0685-5 (hc)
ISBN: 978-1-4917-0686-2 (e)

Library of Congress Control Number: 2013916689

Printed in the United States of America.

iUniverse rev. date: 11/12/2013

Contents

Preface

After giving countless speeches and talks to business school classes and corporations from the West Coast to the East Coast, with requests from my audiences, executives, and friends, I came to realize that if I could put what I have learned into a book, it would benefit a great many people.

Doing one's homework is critical for any business trip and especially important for travel to China or elsewhere in Asia. In addition to standard preparations, it is important to be able to function comfortably within the culture of the country or region that one is visiting. Unfortunately, few companies provide guidance or training on culture to their employees traveling outside of their home countries—even though understanding local mores can often influence the success of a business trip.

Having traveled millions of miles over the past forty years, I quickly envisioned a book that a business executive could pick up in the airport. He or she could spend a few hours on the long twelve- or sixteen-hour flight going over the book. By the time the flight landed in Beijing or Shanghai, that reader would be quite well prepared to make his or her business trip more meaningful.

Some of the proverbs and sayings included in this book may not make sense to Western readers at first glance. This is exactly why one should learn to appreciate the "doesn't make much sense" culture of another country. Although this book was intended for Western business executives, it will equally benefit all those who wish to enhance their relationships with Chinese and Asian friends, family, and colleagues. In addition, this book can also help Asians living in the Western world, by allowing them to realize what they need to *not* do to adapt to Western culture. American-born Chinese, or "ABC," and Canadian-born Chinese, or "CBC," as they are called, have grown up in the United States and Canada under their Chinese parents. They may not be aware that they too have been the recipients, to some degree, of Chinese cultural upbringing. This book will help make them conscious of some specific matters. For example, their Chinese parents, having grown up in China, were taught to always be quiet in the presence of the elderly and in front of a group of people. This upbringing is passed on to their ABC/CBC children. Hence, the children may tend to be rather quiet in the classroom or meeting room and may not be as outgoing as their Western peers.

Finally, you will see that within this book the term "Asian culture" is sometimes used instead of "Chinese culture." This is because Chinese culture is a specific part of the larger Asian culture, and there are differences between Asia as a whole and China specifically. When "Asian" is used, this means that the information also applies to the larger region of Asia.

It is also important to note that mainland Chinese use the simplified Chinese characters, and the Taiwan and overseas Chinese use the traditional or conventional Chinese characters. One will find that many conventional Chinese characters are also incorporated into the Japanese and Korean languages, which evolved from the ancient history of China.

It is advisable while doing business with China to not discuss political situations between China and Taiwan or anything regarding religion. This is no different from the usual recommendation in any country or in any social gathering; my own parents, like others, coached us to avoid discussing politics and religions in all family and social gatherings.

I for one do not like to read long and thick books. That is why I made this book easy to read and included artwork and pictures. As they say, a picture is worth a thousand words. This not only makes the book easy to understand and remember but also makes it fun to read.

Acknowledgments

There are so many old Chinese sayings that we can almost pick one for any occasion we experience in our daily life. One of my favorites says that when you go to take a drink of water from a stream, you should think about and appreciate where it originated. This helps me to keep perspective and to never forget where I came from.

There have been many long book acknowledgments, and I am happy to go for a record because there are many, many people who have meant a great deal to me, particularly those who have helped and guided me over the years. Some may not even realize that they have inspired me at some point in my life.

My eternal gratitude goes, of course, to my parents. They fled from China to Myanmar, where I grew up and where we had to learn not only the language of a foreign country but also how to blend into Burmese society. We had to watch the way that we ate, dressed, spoke, and acted to conform to our neighbors' behavior. I'm most grateful to my mom, who had the courage to walk out of our home when my dad insisted on taking me out of college to help him run his company. She would not let any of her eight children grow up without a college degree. A year later, political changes led to nationalization of my father's business, which would have left me without a job as well as without an education. Instead, with little in the way of resources, my parents helped me get to Taiwan.

My life would not have been the same if I had not grown up in a large family of brothers and sisters, all of whom helped and challenged me in getting used to living in a large, loving, and competitive environment. My special appreciation goes to Cora and Len for their funding of my education while I studied at National Taiwan University, living off Cora's monthly Can$30 check, and to Linda and Harry for sponsoring my permanent residence application, which led to my obtaining US citizenship.

My mentors and my cultural teachers had to be Larry Belsky and Dodge Chu. They are two of the greatest bosses I have ever known. They taught me what I needed to know to survive when I first landed in the United States for graduate school in Boston. My fourteen years at Wang Labs I owe to Dr. and Mrs. An Wang, Fred and Courtney Wang, John Cunningham, Paul Guzzi, Harry Chou, Chauncey Chu, Richard Leung, and later John Chambers and Joe Tucci, who, through their respect for Asian culture, excelled in their leadership of a great company. Of particular mention are the two western region team members Alan Beauchamp and Carolyn Prono, whose help and support enabled me to speedily learn US culture, which led to our successful turnaround of Wang Lab's western region.

My gratitude for the next stage of my learning goes to Les Alberthal, Jeff Heller, Mal Gudis, Jim Young, Coley Clark, Garry Moore, Paulette Eberhart, Barry Sullivan, John Harris, Robb Rasmussen, and my team at EDS Asia Pacific region. My special thanks to Mark Travis, Steve Leakey, Kent Billingsley, Jerry Ha, Raymond So, Frank Liu, Cecilia Tam, Mike Butcher, Eddie Soo, Jane Lim, Mickey Austin, Bob Young, Harry Chuang, James Tay, David English, and Steve Smith, who made a major sacrifice in his career in moving to Singapore to learn to be a country manager. Of particular importance to our team's building of a billion-dollar business in the Asia Pacific region was my COO,

Pete Mefford. Pete was formerly the CIO of EDS Corporation. When he took charge of the delivery services in our region, not only did our business grow at a quantum-leap pace, but our customer satisfaction rating shot up also. That truly allowed me to sleep better at night.

All of those who exercised their willingness to live in a foreign country and learn the local culture to excel are successes today. During my nine years at EDS and three years after, Jean Salata from Hong Kong, Dr. Phil Miller from Pittsburgh, Mathew Miao from Taiwan, and my good friend Dean Brown, former premier of South Australia, were among my teachers. Their humility and their down-to-earth attitudes speak for their successes.

My next expression of gratitude goes to T. W. Liu, the founder of iSoftStone, whose trust and friendship have allowed me to help the company expand in the United States. Without the introduction by my good friend Jiadong Qu, I would not have met T.W. and later Tim Liu. The successes in iSoftStone's acquisitions and the achievement of phenomenal growth of these companies in the United States made me a firm believer in the understanding of culture as a key constituent of success.

It was my speeches given to the Chinese Microsoft Employee Network (CHIME), thanks to Yuying Mesaros, that caught the interest of numerous Microsoft employees. During those sessions, I was fortunate to meet Kate Ou, who was a board member of CHIME and is now my coauthor. With her encouragement, along with the support of my good friend and partner Dennis Smith, I was energized to write this book.

I wish to also thank Steve Ballmer and Dr. Qi Lu of Microsoft for giving their support to the Asia members of HYSTA, which led me to the opportunity to serve on the HYSTA/CGSA board. This engagement made me realize how important it is for Asians to learn Western culture to be better equipped for their future careers.

This book is enlivened by the great artwork of my good and talented friend Dave Stephens. I am grateful to Dave for the time he spent learning Chinese culture in our weekly meetings, so that he could express the culture's depth through each piece of artwork that he created. Dave's wife Danielle contributed organizational and management skills and designed the book cover; they brought perfect teamwork to this book.

My special thanks go to Lena Miao, Kate's daughter, and Darcy Smith, Dennis's daughter, for their valuable help and corrections.

I wish to express my deep appreciation to my children Jackie and Jeff, Kathy and Joeri, and Jeff and Cynthia and their mom, Christine, for their input, criticisms, suggestions, and backing throughout the three years I spent writing this book.

Last but not least, I am indebted to the support of my wife Ruth, whose untiring patience and cheering kept me going to completion.

History

China is one of the world's oldest civilizations, dating back to the Neolithic era. Early records indicate that the history of China as a nation, founded around the Yellow River, dates back to the Xia Dynasty in 2100 BC. For approximately 4,000 years of its 4,200-year history, China was governed by dynastic rule, and much of the nation's culture, philosophy, and literature was developed during the Zhou Dynasty, between 1045 and 256 BC.

The key precepts of Chinese culture discussed in this book are largely derived from its history of dynastic rule. Chinese value systems, built around the importance of maintaining a low profile and embracing hardship and the importance of education, integrity, and most important, respect, are intrinsically tied to the way Chinese society evolved under dynastic governance. Understanding this historical truth is important for developing sensitivity to and appreciation of many aspects of Chinese culture.

Connecting East and West!

The world will be a little better ...

Dear Eveline,

Being brought up in the best of both worlds of East + West, You will be the Role Model for my book.

Enjoy and hope you can pick up a few more ideas.

Love - Uncle Ed

Dec 24" 2013

Chapter 1: Historic Originals

THE BOOK OF CHANGE

I CHING

易经

I-Ching

Dating back to 2000 BC, the *I-Ching* is China's oldest extant book of divination. The term "I-Ching" means "Book of Changes." It is an extensive book of more than six thousand pages.

During the Warring States period, the text of the *I-Ching* was reinterpreted as a system of cosmology and philosophy that subsequently became intrinsic to Chinese culture. The text of the *I-Ching* is a set of oracular statements, presented in sixty-four sets of six lines, called hexagrams, many of which are still in use.

Lao Tzu

Lao Tzu is known as the founder of the Chinese philosophy of Taoism (or Daoism). According to legend, Lao Tzu was a mystic philosopher in sixth century BC and the keeper of the archives at the imperial court. He was also thought to be the teacher of Confucius and had many disciples.

When he was eighty years old, Lao Tzu set out for the western border of China, toward Tibet. At the border, a guard, Yin Xi, asked Lao Tzu to record his teachings before he left. For three days he composed a book of all his wisdom in five thousand characters and eighty-one chapters. This composition, known as *Tao Te Ching*—a title that literally means "way," "virtue," and "canon"—is considered in Taoism "The Canon of the Way and the Virtue."

孔子

Confucius

Confucius, China's greatest teacher and philosopher, was born in 551 BC and died in 479 BC. His father died when he was three years old, and he was raised by his mother in poverty. Through the trust of the emperor, his principles were implemented throughout China, and the principles espoused by Confucius are the basis of many Chinese beliefs.

He championed strong family loyalty, ancestor worship, and respect for the elderly. His teachings emphasized self-cultivation and emulation of moral exemplars. He was also the designer of Chinese etiquette in daily behavior.

One of his most notable sayings is "Do not do unto others what you do not want done unto you," which is very similar to a precept found in Western culture.

Mencius

Mencius, one of Confucius's top students, played a key role in the dissemination of Confucius's teachings, establishing the foundation for many key tenets of Chinese culture.

Mencius's own upbringing reflected the importance placed on learning by his great teacher. Like most Chinese mothers throughout ancient history, Mencius's mother deemed education to be of utmost importance to her child's upbringing. When Mencius was a child, his mother relocated their household three times in order to provide him with the optimal environment for nurturing and learning. Living near a cemetery and butcher house led to imitation of and unwanted influence by the neighboring trades. The family finally moved to a school neighborhood, which contributed to his becoming one of the nation's famous scholars.

Emperor Qing Shi-Huang

Qin Shi Huang

Qin Shi Huang was the first emperor to unify China. Under his leadership, the Warring States (Han, Zhao, Yan, Wei, Chu, and Qi) were combined to make China a single nation in the year 220 BC.

He is known as one of the most ruthless emperors in China's history. Among his many dictates was the burning of books and burying of scholars alive to ensure stability. At the expense of many lives, Qin initiated the construction of the Great Wall of China, the Terracotta Army of soldiers in Xian, and the construction of an extensive road system across China.

Sun Tzu

Sun Tzu was an ancient Chinese military general, strategist, and philosopher who lived around 480 BC and served King Helu of Wu.

His book *The Art of War* was based on his tested expertise and is still considered by generals and business executives worldwide to be a classic standard for dealing with and managing conflict.

The first emperor of a unified China, Qin Shihuang, credited the book as invaluable in ending the age of Warring States.

More recently, General Norman Schwarzkopf used Sun Tzu's *Art of War* during Desert Storm in the use of deception and speed while attacking the enemy's weaknesses. Many Japanese companies have leveraged Sun Tzu's teachings for their business success.

It has been reported that *The Art of War* was first introduced into Europe in the eighteenth century. The first copy was published in Paris in 1772, a German version appeared in 1778, and many other European countries published translations thereafter.

Sun Tzu's famous strategy was "know yourself, know your enemy; there lies the strategy for victory!"

Chapter 2: Cultural Forces

Respect

Respect is one of the central precepts of Confucian ideology. Individuals are encouraged at all times to respect those who have greater age or social status and to treat their guests with courtesy and kindness. In Asia, children are taught to respect their elders and obey their parents. At home, the father is usually considered the head of the family. In the workplace, employees are taught to respect their superiors and obey their instructions.

Chinese people are generally obedient in this manner because they believe that their superiors will watch out for them and help boost their success. These practices can be traced back to ancient China, where the populous revered the emperor and did his bidding and expected benevolent treatment in return.

The concept of respect also relates to another prominent Chinese cultural element: saving face. Saving face for another in public is a form of courtesy and respect Chinese give to each other. Many of the cultural mores in Asian culture are ultimately based on a desire for all individuals to "save face," which people achieve by showing respect and avoiding situations that would cause another individual to feel that he or she has lost respect in some way.

Listening with the Heart and the Ears

Traditionally, Chinese characters are formed through the assembly of a few individual characters. Dissection of the character for the word "listen" shows that it is formed as a combination of the characters for "ear," "eyes," "king" (representing priority), and "heart."

When one is listening, one should pay close attention to concentrating with the heart and eyes in addition to one's ears.

This has a specific application in business meetings. In meetings, Chinese executives usually pay full attention to what Western visitors have to say. It is the right Chinese etiquette for these visitors to pause after their initial message and wait for the Chinese executives to speak. Sometimes it will take a few seconds—maybe five to eight seconds—before the Chinese executives begin their message. This is a silent period that Western executives are not used to, but they need to be patient. When listening, it is a good gesture for the junior Western executives to take notes to show respect.

Kung Fu versus Boxing

Chinese culture is very different from Western culture, and perhaps a way to illustrate the difference between the two cultures is to compare two popular sports: kung fu and boxing.

The reason for choosing these two sports as an example is that these are two confrontational onstage sports from East and West that are performed in the presence of a large audience. The way each opponent behaves and how they treat each other shows the distinctive culture differences between East and West.

Asian culture places great emphasis on conservatism, humility, subtlety, and a low profile. This can be observed in many aspects of Asian life but nowhere as much as in the traditional practice of kung fu. Unlike in its Western counterpart, boxing, the goal in kung fu is not to attack the opponent using severe or harsh body blows. Instead, competitors aim to execute precise movements that show advantage and skill without inflicting harm to their opponent. When the match has been decided, the competitors are still standing and bow respectfully to one another.

In Chinese culture, there is a phrase known as 点到为止—"stop where you touch"—which generally means that once the winner is known, there is no need to continue fighting to cause embarrassment to the opponent.

This same concept applies to how people interact with one another generally.

Feng Shui

Feng shui (Chinese geomancy) is an integral part of everyday living for many Chinese people. The words "feng" and "shui" literally mean "wind" and "water," representing the relationship of our daily lives with the environment. The art of feng shui began as early as 5000 BC with the Yangshao (仰韶文化) and Hongshan (红山文化) cultures.

Many Chinese and Asians believe in the significance of feng shui and apply the concept when deciding the locations of buildings, the sites of important events, and the places of marriage and burial. It is common belief that a good feng shui site will have positive influence and bring peace and harmony to married couples and future generations to come. The feng shui master checks the birth dates and zodiac signs of a couple to ensure their feng shui will be in harmony, including a study of the couple's "Five Elements" (gold, wood, water, fire, and earth). Traditionally, the Chinese sought tomb sites that were backed by mountains and faced water. Such a site represented a solid backing with a great future flow of water, thus ensuring blessings and good fortune would be bestowed on their children for many generations to come.

In China and many Asian countries, such as Hong Kong, Taiwan, Singapore, and Macau, most business office renovations or relocations involve a feng shui master's calculation of the zodiac sign and the birth date and time of day of the CEO or the top executive, so that the layout of his or her office can be designed accordingly. This is considered to be an essential action to ensure the prosperity of the business and the harmony and safety of the employees. It is even more critical to have the feng shui master review and approve the business's acquisition of real estate or another company as part of due diligence.

Yin and Yang

"Yin and yang" literally means "shadow and light." The symbol is widely used and has deep significance as the foundation of Taoism and other Chinese philosophies.

The concept of yin and yang is often used to illustrate the idea that two things that are polar opposites are actually very closely connected with each other. Many examples of yin and yang exist in the natural world, such as female and male, darkness and light, and negative and positive.

There is a common misconception that yin and yang represent evil and good, but this is not the case. Yin and yang should be viewed not as two opposing forces but rather as two forces that interact and feed off each other to contribute to a greater whole. Yin and yang cannot exist separately, just as we would not be able to understand the idea of light if there were no darkness.

Red

For the Chinese, the color red represents luck and good fortune. Red is the primary color used at weddings, birthday celebrations, and banquets. It is also customary to use red for gift wrapping and New Year's envelopes. Promotional materials for special occasions and events also frequently use red.

Colors such as black and white are not often used because they represent death and are typically used at funeral occasions.

Lucky and Unlucky Numbers

The Chinese are very sensitive to numbers. In the Chinese language, the number eight is pronounced "ba." This is similar to the pronunciation for "prosperity" and "growth" in Chinese, and thus eight is considered a lucky number. Similarly, the number three rhymes with the words for "living," "alive," "fresh," and "revitalization." The number nine sounds like the words for "longevity" and "eternal." These three numbers are particularly auspicious.

The importance of these numbers is reflected in the premium that is sometimes paid for house numbers, license plates, and so on. Items that have these numbers are usually priced at a premium. For example, a license plate number of 888 or 333 in Hong Kong might be auctioned off for over US$50,000 and license plate numbers have sold for as much as US$320,000!

By contrast, the number four is considered unlucky because it sounds like the Chinese word for "death." As a result, it is not uncommon to see buildings with no fourth, fourteenth, or twenty-fourth floors.

The Chinese Zodiac

The zodiac, an astrological diagram divided into a twelve-year cycle with each year represented by a different animal, is a core element of Chinese culture. This twelve-year cycle repeats over and over. For example, a father who shares the sign of Dragon with his son will be at least two cycles or twenty-four years older, if not thirty-six (or another multiple of twelve) years older.

Chinese people relate the year of their birth to the animals in the zodiac, and typically people pay respect to their elder or more seasoned counterparts. For example, someone whose birth zodiac sign is Ox will be one year (or one plus a multiple of twelve years) older than someone whose sign is Tiger.

Often during social banquets, Chinese executives will exchange zodiac signs with visitors to determine the toasting order by seniority.

Many Chinese fables derive from the zodiac. Special characteristics or personalities are attributed to each zodiac animal. Oftentimes parents will send soon-to-be-married couples to a feng shui master to have their zodiacs analyzed, to determine whether the match will produce a harmonious, happy marriage. In some companies, the zodiac signs of hired executives are studied as one signal of an individual's compatibility with a company's management or owners. A similar process is sometimes applied to board members and partners.

The Dragon

Among the twelve animals of the zodiac, the Dragon—symbolic of the emperor—reigns supreme.

The Dragon is a mythical creature thought to live in heaven and carry out heaven's orders. In ancient times, the emperor's robes and other personal items were always emblazoned with dragons. In the emperor's palace in Beijing's Forbidden City, there is a carved marble dragon over two hundred feet long. It is located immediately in front of the place where the emperor would give his daily messages.

The year 2012 was the year of the Dragon and therefore was considered a year of good luck for weddings, births, moves to new residences, the founding of companies, and so on. As a result, 2012 was a great year for Chinese hotels and banquet halls, which were reserved for weddings throughout the entire year.

Classroom

Honoring one's teacher is seen as an important virtue in Chinese culture, particularly in a classroom setting.

Confucian doctrine dictates behavior in the classroom. For over 2,500 years, Chinese students have been taught that obedience is paramount and that by remaining silent, a student shows respect. By speaking up, the student might risk posing a challenge to the teacher in a way that causes the teacher to lose face.

By contrast, students are encouraged to ask questions in a Western classroom. In this environment, students have more freedom to discuss what they are learning, and students are rewarded for active participation.

Education

A famous Confucian saying is 学而不厌, 诲人不倦—"never be content with what you have learned; never be impatient when teaching someone something you have already learned."

As noted earlier, for most Chinese families, it would be difficult to overstate the importance placed on education. Parents commonly place all other priorities behind their commitment to helping a son or daughter in the pursuit of a quality education.

The importance of education dates back to ancient times, when the nation's top tiers of scholars were appointed to governorships and other related important positions based on their performance in annual imperial examinations. As a result of these thousands of years of national examination practices, all citizens, regardless of whether they are poor or rich, are given an equal chance to participate. This has been the driving force encouraging emphasis on education, allowing the future generation of each family an opportunity to uplift their future.

The emphasis placed on education by Chinese parents is remarkable in comparison with the parents of Western counterparts.

Ninja

A ninja or 忍者 is an individual with extreme patience and the ability to endure discomfort. The ninja is a common icon of Asian culture, often representing the saying "no pain, no gain."

To become a ninja, one must persevere through extreme physical, mental, and emotional trials and challenges, a trait that is aptly represented in the Chinese character 忍, which when split into parts depicts the character for "knife" above the character for "heart." Even with a knife in the heart, a true ninja is able to endure.

The admiration in Asian culture for ninjas is consistent with the belief held by many that one must go through extreme hardship to become a model of success.

Chapter 3: Business and Meetings

Business Cards

For the Chinese, business cards represent a very important type of exchange when two individuals meet in a business context. The exchange of business cards should take place as part of the initial greeting when you are interacting at a business event or function. It is best for the business card to be bilingual, clearly noting the individual's name, title, and company. When exchanging business cards and addressing a new Asian acquaintance, there are several important guidelines to keep in mind.

- o Stand with both feet close together and make a slight bow of the head.

- o Present your card (with the translated Chinese side up) to the other party using both hands (an important sign of respect).

- o Upon receiving the other party's card, examine it carefully—it is often considered nice to make small conversation about the location of his or her office, to show interest. And it is considered impolite to write on another person's business card.

It is very important to keep a steady supply of business cards on hand at all times. You will be expected to exchange business cards at all business functions with Asians. Running out of cards suggests a lack of understanding of local culture and an inability to reciprocate this important exchange.

Dress Code/Attire

The dress code in Chinese culture tends to be more formal than in the West. Most business functions require a suit and a tie for men. For women, a business dress or proper pantsuit with conservative colors is always appropriate. It is recommended that excessive or loud jewelry be avoided.

It is also important to keep in mind that the Chinese definition of "casual" is different from the Western definition. Whereas Westerners may view casual dress as a T-shirt, jeans, and sneakers, a casual event in Chinese culture would typically require a dress shirt, trousers, and dress shoes. Dressing appropriately is very important when attending functions because certain venues may refuse entry if one doesn't adhere to the customary dress code, resulting in an embarrassing situation for both the guest and the host.

When in doubt, it is better to dress up rather than down.

Figure 1.1 Vehicle Seating Arrangement

Limo/Taxi Seating Protocol for Arrivals

When conducting business in Asian countries, it is not unusual for a client to send a specially ordered taxi or limousine to transport visiting executives to a designated meeting place. When this happens, there are some important rules to keep in mind in terms of seating protocol. The visiting highest-ranking executive should sit in the back right seat (diagonal to the driver). The next-ranking visitor should sit in the back left (behind the driver), and the next visitor should sit in the front, next to the driver. Upon arrival, this seating order will allow the client to know the order of rank among the visiting executives. Sitting in the VIP 1 position will also allow the guest to exit the vehicle with the least effort.

It is important to observe these seating positions to avoid embarrassing situations. Often, Westerners visiting Asian clients do not follow these arrangements and sit wherever is most convenient. This may result in an awkward greeting situation if the most highly ranked executive is not seated in the VIP 1 seat.

Limo/Taxi Departure Courtesy

Following a business visit, Asian clients will sometimes see off their guests and wait by the curb for the visiting party to get in the car and leave. At this point, it is quite common for the Western visitors to strike up conversation inside the car and forget that the client is still waiting outside to see them off.

It is both polite and very important for the departing party to roll down the windows and wave good-bye as the car is making its departure. This ends the visit respectfully.

Meetings

In Western culture, business meetings are typically held for two reasons: for informational purposes or to solicit opinion and input from a team for the purposes of making a decision and building a consensus. In Asian cultures, meetings are generally informational only. Because of the tendency to show respect through deference, there is often little dialogue.

Chinese team members are much less likely to question the leader or to voice opposing opinions, and they believe that this helps a meeting run more smoothly. Chinese people will rarely say no directly and are more likely to smile and stay quiet. Although this may be frustrating for Westerners who are trying to use a meeting as a more dynamic interchange of ideas, managers need to be aware of the tendency for Asians to shun active participation in a meeting. This means that managers need to be skilled at soliciting ideas and building consensus outside of a meeting setting.

Seating

When conducting business or building friendships with the Chinese, one of the most essential social activities to engage in is a shared meal. Having lunch or dinner is usually the best way to meet senior officials or executives or your Chinese counterparts. It is a good way to meet in a non-office environment.

Seating positions are critical to a positive outcome of a lunch or dinner meeting. The seating plan should follow Chinese protocol. Host 1 should sit in the position facing the room's entrance. Host 2 should sit opposite of Host 1. So if Host 1 is sitting in the twelve o'clock position, then Host 2 should sit in the six o'clock position, and Host 3 and Host 4 should sit in the nine o'clock and three o'clock positions, respectively. The VIP Guest 1 should sit to the right of Host 1, and the VIP Guest 2 should sit on the left. When in doubt, one can always ask for advice from the Chinese organization's administrative contact. He or she will be glad to direct people into the proper seating positions.

High-ranking Chinese government leaders will often meet their visitors in the leader's guesthouse. Usually they meet in a large living room with many sofas. In this case, the two most senior representatives from each side will sit facing each other on the center sofas. The rest of the members will sit according to descending rank within their own organization.

Bill Paying at Restaurants

Following a meal in a restaurant, it is not uncommon to see Asian diners fighting over the bill. This is because paying for a meal is seen as a sign of respect in Asian culture. In doing so, the host (or bill payer) gives his guests great "face."

Attention to Details Is a Sign of Respect

Chinese people have many small gestures in everyday life that show respect to their elders, senior officials, guests, and important people in their lives.

Gestures such as opening and holding doors, allowing seniors to take their seats first, and pouring beverages or serving food for guests are all examples of showing respect. Similarly, it is not uncommon to see two people fighting over who will let the other person onto the elevator first.

These actions are all seen as small but important ways of showing respect.

Saving Face

Chinese individuals are typically very conscious of "saving face," both for themselves and for those they respect. People respect individuals who are gentle, friendly, and considerate of others. Asians will rarely deliberately cause another person to "lose face" except under the most stressful of circumstances and will, in most situations, make every effort to preserve the good image of a friend or colleague.

Generally, people avoid delivering negative comments face-to-face when interacting with business associates, friends, or relatives. Engaging in obnoxious, loud, or blunt behavior or anything negative in front of people is looked upon as disrespectful and as poor behavior. The only exceptions can be for family members, people with whom you are very close, or people toward whom you want to deliberately express your anger or dislike. For example, when asked by the host of your opinion on her cooking or her flower arrangements, positive feedback in front of other guests is appropriate.

The predisposition to save face can sometimes make everyday interactions challenging, and thus, one-on-one exchanges are encouraged when a person is seeking genuine and honest feedback.

No Direct Rejection

Confucian precepts dictate that it is important to always maintain a harmonious atmosphere when meeting guests or business associates, to avoid making others uncomfortable, and to ensure that all parties can save face in most situations.

This propensity to ensure harmonious meetings often comes at the expense of clarity or openness and can frequently be a source of confusion for Westerners, who may get the wrong impression.

When meeting with an Asian or Chinese client, one should not automatically assume the mood to be positive or promising because the Chinese will not deliver negative news (such as a rejection) in a direct, face-to-face manner.

Westerners commonly misinterpret gestures or comments that would otherwise be positive indicators in their own culture and should be sensitive to this in negotiations with Chinese counterparts. For example, when proposing a deal with a Chinese firm, Western executives may be respectfully hosted while visiting the clients, given souvenir gifts, and seen away at the airport. However, after they return home, they may receive messages that their proposal has not been accepted.

Don't Ask Uncomfortable Questions

The practice of asking questions is very different in Chinese culture than it is in Western culture. And the answers received are interpreted differently.

For example, if a Chinese business contact or friend is hosting a party and someone asks if he or she can wear jeans and sneakers, this can create a very awkward situation.

Foreigners are regarded as guests when they visit a Chinese company or home, so Chinese hosts generally will say yes to their requests. However, the Chinese "yes" is not equivalent to the Western "yes" and carries other possible meanings.

For instance, while a guest at a Chinese home, one should not ask whether smoking is allowed. The Chinese host will most likely say yes. But this will no doubt cause major problems at home after the guests depart.

The best way to avoid awkward situations is to ask another Chinese friend or colleague whether it is appropriate to bring up your request.

Silence

The Chinese typically stay quiet in meetings, in the classroom, and in public settings to avoid being "the nail that sticks out." This quietness can be traced back to ancient times in China.

For thousands of years, China employed a dynastic system. It was a typical practice for the current emperor to exact revenge on the previous emperor and his followers. The outcome usually resulted in death or, if the emperor was feeling generous, exile.

Based on this practice, members of the public learned to keep a low profile and stay quiet to avoid attracting attention. This type of behavior is in direct contrast to the Western tendency to speak up.

This concept is taught to Chinese children when they begin their education and carries through their adult interactions. Children are taught to stay silent in the classrooms and to be totally obedient to the teachers. Thus, in all classrooms, mostly one-way communication is practiced unless a student is asked to speak about a topic.

Seeking True Feedback

Chinese actively avoid giving conflicting opinions, particularly to their bosses or teachers. This behavior often is difficult for Western managers.

As a result of an upbringing wherein most Chinese learn to exercise a quiet and respectful demeanor in social settings, most Chinese individuals avoid giving opposing opinions in public meetings and business interactions. If the meeting leader asks a question or is looking for feedback, Asians will generally not have much response except a few words of consent or a nod, meaning "I hear you" but not necessarily "I agree with you."

The most effective way to get honest feedback is to arrange one-on-one meetings where individuals will be more likely to express what they are really thinking.

Chapter 4: Social Encounters

Handshake

The Asian greeting style is more formal than the Western greeting style. Asians typically greet each other with a bow or a nod of the head. The degree of the bow depends on the importance or seniority of the other party and the circumstances of the occasion. If two individuals are familiar with one another, they will often nod as they approach.

By contrast, Westerners typically greet each other with a firm handshake. Because Asians are less comfortable making physical contact with strangers, their handshakes may seem weak. This is often misinterpreted as lack of confidence.

In recent years, with globalization, Asians have become more comfortable shaking hands, and it has become a more acceptable greeting practice, particularly when meeting with Westerners.

When a Westerner meets with a Chinese person for the first time, the Chinese person does not expect the Westerner to bow. The Chinese person will be prepared to offer a handshake when one is initiated by the Westerner.

Eye Contact

Confucian principles deem direct eye contact with a superior to be highly disrespectful. In fact, in the ancient days, looking directly into the eyes of the emperor could result in a death sentence for an unfortunate subject!

As a result, in Asian culture, eye contact is viewed somewhat differently than in Western culture. Westerners often misinterpret a lack of eye contact as a sign of rudeness or lack of confidence when, in fact, the reality is that by avoiding eye contact, an Asian counterpart is actually showing a sign of respect.

If two Chinese people of the same status or ranking meet, they will usually make direct eye contact. However, if an individual is meeting someone of a higher ranking, such as a business executive or government official, that individual will frequently bow to show respect and to avoid direct eye-to-eye contact.

Harmony and Sharing

Harmony is an important Confucian principle that dominates many aspects of Chinese culture. This is perhaps best depicted in eating situations.

Asians tend to embrace the use of circular tables, bowls, and plates. They believe this setup helps to establish a warmer atmosphere and is generally more harmonious, the main reason being that circular shapes do not have sharp corners that disrupt smooth flow of boundaries. On the other hand, Westerners tend to make greater use of square or rectangular dining sets.

Sharing is also an important aspect of establishing harmony. When eating together, the Chinese tend to share their food family-style. Because there is typically more than enough rice and other food to go around, it is not uncommon for the Chinese to invite last-minute guests to join them for meals.

Chinese Banquet

If you do business in China, you will no doubt attend a Chinese banquet during your visit, at the end of it, or both. Banquets are great opportunities to build friendships, get acquainted, or celebrate, and the variety of dishes is an important part of the banquet.

Most banquets are held in a very formal manner with invitations, seating arrangements, and formal dishware. These banquets serve many courses of food—usually eight, ten, or twelve—in order to show the host's goodwill.

Often there will be roasted pig, chicken, fresh vegetables, fish, and noodles to represent prosperity, a good harvest, and longevity.

It is important to pace yourself when eating so that you do not stop halfway through. This can be interpreted as a sign that you are upset or offended in some way. Toasts are also part of the routine, adding to the fun.

One aspect of the meal that commonly surprises Westerners is that when fish, chicken, duck, and roasted pig are served, the head and tail of each of the animals are usually included. Contrary to Western custom, the Chinese believe in serving "complete," from head to toe, to show full offering and that they are holding nothing back. This practice also represents wholehearted goodwill of partnership, with 100 percent commitment.

Don't Finish Everything on Your Plate

This adage is important to remember when dining with your Chinese friends. Because the Chinese are very hospitable to their guests, they want to be sure that no one leaves a meal hungry.

If a guest finishes all the food on his or her plate, this indicates to the host that he or she is still hungry, in which case the host will continually refill the plate to avoid losing face.

To indicate that one is full and satisfied, one should leave a small amount of food on the plate.

Guanxi

"Guanxi" literally means "relationship," but the idea of guanxi goes much deeper, possessing significant cultural implications.

It is often difficult for strangers to build trust. In any culture, trust comes with time and effort, and the outcome is not always guaranteed. Beyond relationship, guanxi implies a moral obligation between two parties and the concept of reciprocity. As such, Chinese people establish guanxi only with parties whom they know and respect.

Guanxi is usually linked back to a person's relatives, school classmates, or others who have served or worked with the person over many years. It is then extended to others in an individual's community through direct or indirect introduction. In a business environment, for example, to pursue a deal with a prospective customer, one will try to seek point of entry by exploring connectivity of guanxi between one's own executive staff and the prospect's executive team.

It is also known that a CEO of a Chinese company will recruit senior executive positions only through his own guanxi network or through someone he trusts.

Patience and Hard Work

In elementary school textbooks in China, students are taught a mythical story in which a young man is traveling in the mountains and encounters an old woman. He asks her what she is doing, and she says she is grinding a large iron rod into a very tiny needle. The man thought the task was impossible, but the old woman replied that anything is possible as long as you are patient and willing to work hard.

This story is often invoked by parents as a lesson to their children that good results will come from hard work and perseverance.

Humility

The Chinese, and most Asians, are known to downplay their capabilities. In Asian culture, staying low-profile and humble is considered virtuous.

Humility and modesty are fundamental maxims of Confucian teaching. Possessing a humble and open-minded attitude is considered important when interacting with others. In fact, the higher ranked an individual is, the more humble he or she is expected to be.

The Chinese strongly believe that "the nail that sticks out gets hammered down."

Gifts and Reciprocity

When visiting Chinese clients or friends, it is customary to bring a small gift. Bringing a small gift is a gesture of goodwill and is consistent with the Chinese desire to make meetings harmonious. For business meetings, one can consider gifting a company T-shirt, chocolates, or a small token from your home city.

When visiting senior officials, it is a good idea to ask ahead of time whether a gift exchange is expected. This can help prevent embarrassing situations.

For first-time meetings, a small gift is recommended. For subsequent visits, one can tailor the gift to that person's interests. Usually the local staff will bring up the need for gift exchange because the Chinese party will provide a heads-up on whether or not there will be one.

It is also a good idea to wrap the gift in bright colors such as red or gold. Do not give flowers because those are often given to the sick and are presented at funerals.

When receiving a gift, the recipient will typically attempt to refuse the gift first before accepting it, to prevent the appearance of being too greedy.

Do Not Open Your Gift in front of Others

In contrast to Western custom, in Chinese culture, people do not typically open gifts in front of the giver or other guests. Since the gift is intended to be personal, it is best opened in private.

In keeping with this practice, Westerners who are recipients of gifts should keep in mind the fact that it could be embarrassing to your Chinese guests if you open your gift in front of them.

Never Lose Your Temper

It is very unusual to see Chinese executives or leaders lose their tempers at meetings where guests are present. In contrast, Westerners sometimes lose their tempers at meetings deliberately, often with the view that an uncomfortable atmosphere can lead to a better outcome. Chinese businesspeople are generally very uncomfortable in this type of setting.

Consistent with this philosophy, the Chinese believe that those in positions of responsibility need to have a very high emotional quotient (EQ).

One important point to remember is that once you lose your temper even just one time, there will be no forgiveness on the Chinese side because you have made them lose face.

天下没有不散的筵席

"There is no banquet that never ends!"

This Chinese phrase comes from the Ming Dynasty author Feng Menglong's collection of stories called *Lasting Words to Awaken the World*. It tells us that no matter how happy something might be, all good things must come to an end.

This is one of the most appropriate sayings to use at the end of a farewell banquet. It allows you to toast to your Chinese host or counterpart and communicate that you have immensely enjoyed the togetherness and are disappointed to see it come to an end. Whatever messages follow this opening remark will flow very smoothly and will be highly appreciated by the Chinese business partners.

Chapter 5: Important Festivals

Chinese New Year

The most celebrated and fun-filled festival of the year for most Chinese is Chinese New Year, which falls on the first day of the lunar year, calculated using the cycles of the moon.

The Chinese calendar combines lunar and solar calendars. It consists of a lunisolar year of twelve months with possible thirteenth and sometimes fourteenth months added to prevent so-called calendar drift. The Chinese calendar is not restricted to China but extends to some of the other Asian countries as well. In everyday business, the Gregorian calendar is used. For any auspicious events such as weddings, the opening of a business, a move to a new house, birthday celebrations, and so on, the Chinese calendar is usually referred to.

Over the past three thousand years, many traditions for celebrating the New Year have evolved. Most Chinese share a common practice of a family reunion dinner on New Year's Eve.

As New Year's Day arrives at midnight, firecrackers are set off to drive away the foul spirits and unlucky tidings of the past year. It is customary to wear new clothes to signify a new start of happiness and good fortune. At the city centers and in company offices, the festival is commemorated with a Dragon or Lion Dance performance that includes strong drumbeats to signify driving bad fortune away and the welcome of a new year.

Red Envelopes

The Chinese are rather direct and straightforward in their gift giving. In the Western world, for special occasions such as Christmas, New Year's, weddings, birthday parties, or baby showers, people usually shop for a unique gift or pick from a preregistered department store list of chosen merchandise. On such occasions, the Chinese typically present a red envelope, which represents good luck. Inside the envelope is a cash gift.

Red envelopes, known as "hong bao" in Mandarin or "lai see" in Cantonese, are ubiquitous during Chinese New Year. Adults give gifts to younger individuals (particularly children and staff members). The dividing line between giver and recipient is generally based on marital status. If one party is married, the couple will be the giver of red envelopes. It is not necessary for red envelopes to be exchanged between people who are single, and neither is it necessary among married couples. The amount gifted depends on a giver's personal financial status and his or her relationship with the recipient. In addition to family members, red envelopes are also given out to subordinates, restaurant managers, waiters, and other people one has interacted with and known throughout the year.

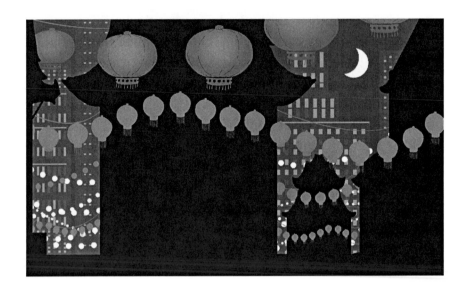

Lantern Festival

The fifteenth day of the first month of the lunar New Year is when people celebrate the Lantern Festival. On this day, most households hang lanterns in front of their house to welcome the first full moon of the year. This is also the day on which the Chinese New Year celebration officially ends.

During this festival, individuals celebrate by seeking to cultivate positive relationships with family, friends, and nature.

The Lantern Festival is known for the gifting and enjoyment of a sweet glutinous rice ball with black sesame, red bean, or lotus seed filling. The Chinese word for these rice balls sounds similar to the phrase "tuan yuan," which is used to represent families gathering together.

During the festival, families and visitors go outdoors to appreciate the varieties of lanterns and to solve lantern-themed puzzles. Historically, the Lantern Festival is known to be the busiest day of the year for matchmakers.

Qingming Festival

The Qingming Festival (Ching Ming or Tomb Sweeping Day) occurs on the fifteenth day of the Chinese spring calendar and usually falls in early April.

On this day, it is customary to visit the tombs of ancestors as well as the more recently deceased. Food, drink, and flowers are brought to the cemetery to pay respect to the departed. After this process, the food and drink are enjoyed either at the cemetery or at a nearby park, signifying a reunion meal with the family.

Some traditional Chinese also believe that the deceased live in another similar world where material goods are essential. Hence, it is a common practice to burn paper money (spirit money), paper houses, cars, televisions, and so on to enhance the quality of life for their ancestors.

Wherever the Chinese are, the tradition of giving thanks and asking for blessings from the forefathers is widely observed on this day.

Dragon Boat Festival

The Dragon Boat or "Duanwu" Festival occurs on the fifth day of the fifth Chinese lunar month. This usually falls on a day in June.

The historic event that started this festival took place in 267 BC and was in remembrance of Qu Yuan, a statesman and poet serving the emperor of the Zhou Dynasty. The emperor, after rejecting Qu Yuan's advice against his partnership with the Qin state, was captured by the Qins. Qu Yuan, in despair, committed suicide by jumping into the Miluo River.

The locals, who admired Qu Yuan's talent and contributions to China, raced in boats in search of him. They also threw sticky rice dumplings into the river to feed the fish so that Qu Yuan would not be harmed. Nowadays, people conduct similar races in dragon-shaped boats and eat sticky rice dumplings in remembrance of Qu Yuan.

Mid-Autumn Festival

The Mid-Autumn Festival or Lunar Festival falls on the full moon that occurs during the eighth month of the Chinese lunar calendar (falling in September or October).

The mythical story of this festival has many versions dating back three thousand years to the Zhou Dynasty. The main version tells the story of Houyi and Chang'e, Houyi's wife. It is said that Houyi became a very powerful king after he shot down nine suns that were about to burn the earth. He eventually grew greedier for power and longed for immortality. Houyi found a pill that promised eternal life. But Chang'e, fearing that the country would forever be ruled by a cruel tyrant (her husband), found the pill and swallowed it herself. She then began to fly into the sky. Houyi was extremely angry and tried to shoot her down, but Chang'e escaped to the moon. It is believed that on a clear day, one can see Chang'e on the moon with a rabbit accompanying her.

Over time people began the tradition of eating moon cakes in remembrance of Chang'e's good deed. Nowadays, families gather together on this night of the full moon and set up tables with moon cakes, fruits, and desserts to celebrate their reunion.

Chapter 6

誰 知 盘 中 餐 粒 粒 皆 辛 苦

"Each grain in your dish is a fruit of hard labor."

This Chinese proverb comes from a Tang Dynasty poem. It tells us it is important to be appreciative of the fact that we can nourish our appetites only because of the efforts of many.

The proverb encourages its reader to be thankful and to realize the value of hard work.

孔 融 讓 梨

"Kong Rong chose the smallest pear."

Kong Rong was a descendant of Confucius. This story comes from the Three Character Classic, a classic for children. It illustrates the importance of humility and the Chinese practice of giving up the best to others.

The Chinese teach their children to make sacrifices and pick a smaller or lesser choice. This sacrifice and show of deference indicates good upbringing and respect to others.

This quotation comes from the story of Kong Rong, who gave away the bigger pears to his brothers and took the smallest one for himself.

先 敬 萝 衣 後 敬 人

"Respect the dress before giving respect to the person."

In Chinese society, people often pay attention to the clothes or outfit that a person is wearing before they notice a person's personality or character.

People who dress better are usually given more leeway in society. They tend to be treated more favorably and will often have advantages over people who dress poorly.

养儿才知父母恩

"We never know the love of our parents until we become parents ourselves."

This maxim is often recited to remind sons and daughters to be grateful to their parents. It suggests that they will fully comprehend their parents' sacrifices and the true extent of their parents' love only when they have children themselves.

In the business context, this saying can also be applied to those who have been promoted to managers, as an expression of appreciation of the responsibility and work pressure such positions carry.

少 壮 不 努 力 老 大 徒 伤 悲

"Laziness in youth spells regret in old age."

This proverb comes from a collection of Yuefu lyric poems compiled in the twelfth century by Guo Maoqian.

Guo's poems illustrate how life is similar to the seasons in nature and how things can be short-lived, affirming the principle that it is best to act soon rather than waiting. This particular proverb encourages individuals to study hard and work diligently in their youth in order to live a fulfilling life in old age.

Starting early will allow efforts to pay off in the long run, a theme seen often.

掘 井 九 仞 功 亏 一 篑

"Digging a well for nine thousand feet and quitting right before you hit water."

An ancient Chinese story tells of a group of people who dug a well nine thousand feet deep in search of water, to no avail. But had they dug only one more foot, they would have reached their objective.

This story is used to encourage people to not give up because success could be just around the corner.

有人辞官归故里,有人连夜赶科场

"There are people who resign and go home, and there are also people who are zealous to apply for those same posts."

In ancient China, governmental positions were the most sought-after and prestigious positions attainable.

Nevertheless, these positions were not for everyone. This proverb reminds us that different people have different aspirations and affirms that when one person leaves a position, there is typically someone else who will wish to fill it.

良药苦口 利于病 忠言逆耳 利于行

"Bitter medicine cures illness."

This Confucian saying avows that the most effective medicine is one that has the most offensive taste.

This aphorism is used both to describe antidotes to illness and when considering feedback or criticism, suggesting that the advice that is hardest to accept may, in fact, be the most valuable.

各人自扫门前雪休管他人瓦上霜

"One should shovel the snow on his own driveway and not mind his neighbor's icy roof."

There is no point in worrying about the frost on someone else's roof when there is snow piling up on your own sidewalk. In this manner, Chinese culture encourages people to mind their own business and not meddle in other people's affairs.

This is appropriate advice in the business world, such as when an executive is communicating to each division manager that the manager should concentrate on achieving his or her own group's target and not criticize or cross over to other departments' shortcomings.

学 如 逆 水 行 舟 不 进 则 退

"Learning is like rowing upstream: if you don't forge ahead, you will be swept downstream."

This saying is used to illustrate the importance of constantly pursuing education.

Just as a boat will be swept downstream if one stops paddling against the current, a person's knowledge will recede if he or she stops making the effort to learn. In the real world, without consistent improvement and determination, one will be swept away by the competition.

人 往 高 处 走 水 往 低 处 流

"Humans strive upward; water flows downward."

Humans should always endeavor for higher ground, for a better life, just like water goes in only one direction—downstream.

This proverb posits that humans are unique, with the ability to improve their lot in life with hard work and initiative.

上 樑 不 正 下 樑 歪

"If the upper pillar is crooked, the base will be warped as well."

Another way to think of this saying is "a crooked stick throws a crooked shadow."

This adage suggests that when there is malfeasance at the top of an organization, generally there is likely to be similar behavior throughout. It stresses that maintaining honesty and integrity at senior levels is the best way to provide role models and encourage appropriate ethical standards throughout an organization.

言多必失

"Talking too much will lead to mistakes."

This saying comes from the ancient Chinese rhetoric works. It is often used to caution people against being too long-winded because one will inevitably let something slip and possibly make a mistake.

Careless talk can lead to trouble. Thus, the general belief is that the less said, the better.

货比三家 不为贵

"Shop three stores to get a good deal."

This is a very popular Chinese saying. Shopping in Chinese culture is different from shopping in Western culture. For thousands of years, the Chinese have bargained in the market for purchases. Although it can be a long and time-consuming process, this old saying suggests that if a shopper is looking for the best deal possible, he or she needs to visit at least three shops.

Similarly, in business one should interview at least three candidates or entertain at least three proposals before a final decision is made to pick the best.

上 得 山 多 终 遇 虎

"When journeying too often into the mountains, one will eventually encounter a tiger."

This idiom is used to warn that someone who takes too many risks is likely to encounter trouble over time.

Chinese leaders use idioms and sayings very often in business and relationship building. This saying might be used, for example, when negotiating with a business counterpart to revise an unfair deal that is hurting one party and when the need for a change in terms of the deal is eminent. Should the situation persist, some drastic outcome might result, which then might hurt both parties.

Another way to think of this saying is "the fish that nibbles at every bait will eventually get caught."

朝 中 无 人 莫 做 官

"When you don't have a mentor near the emperor, don't take a government post outside the palace."

In ancient China, taking a government post outside the palace was very dangerous if you did not have a protector within the emperor's group of officials.

Without such support, it could be hard to make progress. In addition, if no one was watching out for you, it would be easy to get into trouble, often with fatal consequences.

This is very critical and even applies to the current world, both East and West. If you don't have a mentor in Washington, DC, the saying warns, don't take an ambassador post, obviously you will not get support from the power base.

In the business world, it is of utmost importance for a regional or international country general manager of a global corporation to have a few mentors or supporters in senior executive positions at the corporate headquarters. Such supporters will be able to look out for him or her in times of need or difficult circumstances, such as when the monthly or quarterly performance of their business unit is below target.

In business terms, this is also known as being set up to succeed or fail, depending on the scenarios.

礼 多 人 不 怪

"One can never be blamed for being too courteous with gifts."

This proverb comes from the Qing Dynasty play *The Revelation of the Officials' True Features*.

It is often used when referring to the Chinese tradition of gift giving. When visiting other people, it is customary to bring the host a small gift as a token of appreciation. Even a small gift is a sign of thoughtfulness and a way to show respect.

Chinese believe that no one will be upset over an overly courteous gesture.

家 和 万 事 兴

"When a family is in harmony, everything will prosper."

This Confucian teaching presents the belief that harmony is a family's most precious commodity. The Chinese believe that when a family is in harmony and working to support one another, all other aspects of their lives will also be prosperous.

Whether in business or other matters, the collective amity of a group will greatly contribute to success. In other words, a company will succeed if the senior management group works in harmony as a team.

有朋自远方来不亦乐乎

"To have friends come from afar is happiness."

This saying comes from the *Analects of Confucius*. Traditionally, visiting from afar meant that one had to make a long and tiring journey, and thus, it was an honor when friends came to visit.

Although travel today is easier, the happiness associated with a visitor from afar is genuine. This phrase is most appropriate to use at the welcome meeting or banquet for visiting business executives from out of town.

The next year...

食色性也

Confucius says, "Food and sex are part of human nature."

As we have seen, the Chinese place great importance on food and sharing. When friends or relatives are visiting, the best way to welcome them is to invite them to share a meal.

When you call on your Chinese friends from out of town, you should not be surprised if they invite you to lunch or dinner. It is important to handle these invitations with sensitivity. If you do not have time for these events, it might seem that you are not giving face to your Chinese friends. There is no good way to decline an invitation to spend time with a Chinese friend, so if you don't have time to meet for breakfast, lunch, or dinner, don't call your Chinese friend.

However, when the Chinese come to visit, Western society does not necessarily share this same practice. Invitations to meals are not always regarded as part of the role of a respectful host. Nevertheless, it is important to keep in mind that reciprocity is not only important to the Chinese, but also part of the system of give-and-take that is ingrained in the culture.

前人种树 後人乘凉

"The first generation plants the tree; the second generation enjoys the shade."

As noted elsewhere in this book, the Chinese are always looking out for their younger generations, and this saying is common. This dictum suggests that the first generation (parents) plants the trees so that the second generation (children) can enjoy the shade.

This saying encourages the current generation to invest in long-term actions that will benefit their children in the future.

In a business context, a founder of a company will include in the company a performance and benefit enhanced system so that a better company will be passed on to the future successors.

真 金 不 怕 火 烧

"Real gold can withstand high heat."

A man or woman of quality and stature, with great determination and motivation, will endure.

This adage is used quite often in complimenting survival of a long and challenging business competition or in complimenting a role model of an employee after a long tenure of service.

It can also be used to thank one's Chinese partner for a solid and harmonious strategic partnership after enjoying a successful performance together.

酒 逢 知 己 千 杯 少 活 不 投 机 半 句 多

"If you click with someone, even a thousand glasses of wine will seem like not enough."

When you enjoy the company of another individual, the time spent together, even "over a thousand glasses of wine," will not seem to be enough.

Conversely, if you never click, then even a short conversation can be difficult to endure.

This is one of the most commonly used phrases among Chinese business leaders at banquet time. This saying is recited when toasting and conversation are going well and toward the latter part of the meal. Saying this will impress Chinese leaders immensely. It will express not only that the Chinese counterparts' involvement in the business is truly welcome but also that the Western executives took great effort to learn the Chinese culture.

十 年 寒 窗 无 人 问 一 朝 成 名 天 下 知

"No one knows when you have been studying hard for ten years, but everyone will know overnight when you have achieved success."

This proverb comes from a Chinese opera piece called *Pipa Ji* dating back to the Yuan Dynasty.

The play tells the story of a young man, Cai Bojie, who left his family to take the ancient imperial examinations in the capital. He studied day and night to achieve the top position in exams. Although no one paid much attention to him during his long and arduous period of studying, he became known and revered widely upon becoming a national scholar.

The moral of the proverb is that every great scholar begins as a young student. It encourages young people to be patient and work hard in the hopes that this effort will yield great wisdom and success in the future.

天将降大任于斯人也 必先苦其心志 劳其筋骨

"When heaven is about to place a great responsibility on a person, one will be tested with great hardships."

This adage from Mencius avers that when a person is about to receive great responsibility from heaven, he or she will be tested with extreme difficulties that may exhaust the body, challenge the spirit, and create setbacks in order to build up his or her character and willpower. It is often recited to urge hardworking people to persist in the face of difficulties or to embrace greater responsibility with the prospect of a brighter future.

严 师 出 高 徒

"The strictest coaches produce champions."

The strict coach who instills the greatest sense of discipline and purpose produces the best results.

Similarly, most Chinese believe that the stricter a parent or teacher is, the more accomplished the child.

The same rule applies in business. It is known that a tough, demanding, and well-disciplined CEO will have a high probability of driving his company to excellence.

谋 事 在 人 成 事 在 天

"Man proposes; heaven disposes."

This precept reminds us that there are no guarantees in life. Chinese culture holds that we should work hard and do our best in all endeavors, leaving the rest up to heaven.

This can be appropriate to use in encouraging members of a proposal team to put in their best effort and leave it to heaven to decide who wins the bid.

养 兵 千 日 用 在 一 时

"Armies are trained for a thousand days to be used in the nick of time."

The historian Li Yan Shou, in compiling the records of the four regimes under the Nan Dynasty, highlighted many axioms that continue to be reflected in Chinese thinking and culture. This dictum emphasizes the importance of preparation for the time of urgent need.

The phrase is often used in motivational speeches for business or when a leader needs to mobilize a team and create a sense of urgency.

斩 草 不 除 根 春 风 吹 又 生

"If you cut the weeds without digging up the roots, they'll grow again when the spring breeze blows."

This is a very common Chinese saying. This idiom tells people that if they set their minds to a task, they should persist and finish it comprehensively. In a similar vein, if there is a problem, people should delve in to get to the root of the issue and try to fix it, or it is likely to resurface.

In the business world this phrase can be used to stress that aggressive actions should be taken to eliminate a competitor's ability to get ahead.

吃 得 苦 中 苦 方 为 人 上 人

"When you work the hardest among the hardworking, you will become the best of the best."

The concept of hard work is integral to Chinese culture, and this is another very common proverb. The Chinese always believe that if you work harder than others, you will become a better person and that he or she who works the hardest will become the best of the best. In other words, the rewards of hard work are multiplied.

三 人 同 行 必 有 我 师

"If three of us walk together, one of them can be my teacher."

This proverb, from the *Analects of Confucius*, illustrates the importance of learning and education.

With a humble and respectful mind-set, there is always something that can be learned from another person, regardless of that person's position.

人 怕 出 名 猪 怕 肥

"A man dreads fame just as pigs dread growing fat."

This proverb comes from the Qing Dynasty novel *A Dream of Red Mansions*, one of the great classics of Chinese literature, and speaks of the possible negative consequences of becoming too famous.

When a pig grows too plump, it will be sent to the slaughterhouse. In a similar vein, a person with great wealth and resources can attract flies that are after his or her money and reputation.

This proverb is used to encourage keeping a low profile so as to avoid unwanted attention.

一山还有一山高

"There are always higher mountains."

This saying tells us that there are always mountains higher than the one you are currently standing on—a metaphor for the never-ending journey to greatness.

This parable conveys that there is always another peak to strive for, encouraging humility along with the knowledge that there will always be greater heights to achieve.

Similarly, in business, one should not be contented with his or her achievements. Knowing that there will be fierce competition from those who are better out in the market, one should always pursue higher ground.

万般皆下品唯有读书高

"The worth of other pursuits is small; learning through the study of books exceeds them all."

This Confucian proverb affirms that when compared with apprentice, vocational, or on-the-job training, learning through studying books is always considered the best choice. People working hard to become farmers, builders, retailers, and so on are considered admirable, but an individual with a profession attained from schools is considered to be noble.

路遥知马力　日久见人心

"As distance tests a horse's strength, so does time reveal a person's heart."

This proverb is from a Yuan Dynasty play known as *Zheng Bao En*. It illustrates the idea of maintaining a friendship through times of adversity. It is easy to be friends with someone during normal and easygoing times, but when trials and tribulations arise, true friends will not leave your side.

True friendship and support should not be fleeting, and the qualities of patience and loyalty should persist through time, regardless of the situation.

行 千 里 路 如 读 万 卷 书

"Traveling a thousand miles is like reading ten thousand books."

According to this proverb, individuals can learn equally well by traveling to new places as through studying at home.

The experience of travel will prompt discovery and enrich a person's knowledge and is the best way to learn about the world and its people.

秀才不出门　能知天下事

"Well informed of events, the scholar need not leave the house."

As we have seen, scholarship is revered above all in Chinese culture.

Lao Zi taught that a learned person could be knowledgeable about what was going on in the world without leaving his home.

知 己 知 彼 百 战 百 胜

"To know one's own strength and the enemy's is the sure way to victory."

This is a key strategy from Sun Tzu's *The Art of War*.

This maxim tells us that the best way to defeat an opponent is to know your own strengths and weaknesses and those of your enemy as well. This knowledge will provide the perspective and understanding needed for success. Though originally intended for war, this principle can be applied to many fields, including business.

四 两 拨 千 斤

"Four ounces of energy can divert the force of a thousand pounds."

This saying is the core principle of the practice of Tai-ji. Although an opponent may attack with great force, a clever person can often divert the assault with a small amount of energy.

In this way, people are encouraged to not always meet things head-on with equal force. Instead, one should consider changing the direction of the aggression by shifting it to a different path.

In a competitive world, this saying is used to urge the team to work "smart" instead of just working hard.

杯水车薪

"Using a cup of water to put out a burning wagon full of wood is next to impossible."

This saying from Mencius's teachings tells the story of a man who tried to put out an entire wagon on fire with just a cup of water, to no avail. It is invoked to emphasize the importance of applying the appropriate resources to address a problem or issue.

In business, the analogy can be applied to the case of an executive taking on too large a business goal or project or a team of technical engineers taking on an impossible product to build.

It can also be used to comment that someone's proposed plan is too far out of range to achieve success.

富不传三代

"Wealth does not pass three generations."

This phrase has origins in one of Mencius's teachings. Chinese history shows that a family's wealth often does not pass beyond three generations. The first generation usually works very hard to build wealth, and the second generation is "born with silver spoons in their mouths" and reaps the benefits. Oftentimes, the third generation ends up squandering the fortune of its forefathers.

天 时 地 利 人 和

"Right time, right place, right people."

This proverb comes from Sun Tzu's *The Art of War*.

The Chinese believe that all good things are made possible in heaven. When auspicious events take place, it is because the conditions are favorable at the right time and the right place with the right people.

One never knows when (timing) and where (place) the great event will occur. By being well prepared, a person greatly enhances his or her chances of success when time and place meet.

船 到 桥 头 自 然 直

"A boat will straighten itself out when it approaches the bridge."

This soothing proverb encourages people to not worry too much about events that are too far in the future.

Things will work themselves out eventually, so there is no need to fret in the present.

天 生 我 才 必 有 用

"Heaven has endowed me with talents for a purpose."

This proverb comes from Tang Dynasty poet Li Bai. It suggests the idea that everyone is endowed with a special talent to be used for a special purpose. When people have lost hope or view life in a negative light, this proverb is used to remind them that they have a purpose and something positive to add to society.

一 样 米 养 百 样 人

"The same rice builds different characters."

This old Chinese saying remarks on how amazing it is that people who eat the exact same rice can be so different in character, style, and personality.

浪 子 回 头 金 不 换

"A prodigal who returns is more precious than gold."

There are few things more upsetting for a family than when a child runs away from home. Though freedom is the goal, the child may suffer many trials and hardships and ultimately find his or her way home.

This proverb advises that a family should welcome the child back with open arms since the child's choice to return was made with a repentant heart, and the child's return is the greatest gift that a parent can ever receive.

In the business world, this phrase can be used to compliment the individual or manager who has succeeded after being given a second chance. It can also be used in relation to someone who has recovered from personal challenges such as rehab.

退一步海阔天空

"Take a step back, and the ocean and sky will come into perspective."

This saying is most commonly used in situations of conflict to encourage people to not let themselves be overtaken by emotion or get too caught up in little details. If one can take a step back, what seems like an insoluble problem might more readily be overcome with calm and perspective.

In problem solving at work, when a manager is too close to a problem, he or she might not see a way to resolve the issue. Taking a step back, the manager might see a better solution from a higher ground.

塞 翁 失 马 奄 知 非 福

"Misfortune might be a blessing in disguise."

There once was an old man who lived close to the Great Wall (or "bian sai") and thus was known as Old Sai.

One day he lost one of his horses from the barn. Everyone in the town felt very sorry for him. But Sai himself did not worry and thought that this situation could perhaps yield something positive.

Sure enough, a few days later, his horse returned, with hundreds of other horses following him, turning Old Sai's loss into a blessing in disguise!

Chinese people often cite this proverb to help provide perspective in situations that seem unfortunate. Even if things appear to be negative or desperate, there is always potential for a silver lining.

知 足 长 乐

"Being content brings happiness."

This saying originates from Lao Zi's *Tao Te Ching* and conveys the idea that having knowledge and wisdom brings happiness derived from a better understanding of the world around you.

Nowadays, the saying supports the idea that being content with one's life will lead to happiness. This happiness is not necessarily one that comes from material wealth. The saying suggests instead that the richest man is not the one who owns the most but the one who wants the least.

冰冻三尺非一日之寒

"A three-foot-thick block of ice was not formed in a day."

The above saying is often used to emphasize the value of persistence and hard work. It can be applied in a business context by an individual who wishes to express that his or her success was not just based on luck but resulted from hard work and dedication.

On the other hand, one can also use this saying to comment on a company that after many years of operations finally failed and filed for bankruptcy. One can say the downfall of that company was not caused by one day's mismanagement.

人算不如天算

"Human predictions are no match for heaven's decisions."

This saying states that humans can make predictions but that their ability will never be able to compare with what heaven dictates as the outcome. Although we can try to predict and plan for what the future will hold, it is ultimately heaven that will make the decision.

In Western civilizations, the term "heaven" is used largely in a Christian context to refer to a place of eternal life, where those who enter dwell with God. However, in China, talking about any religion other than Buddhism or Daoism is taboo, and understanding this is important. In the sense of this proverb, "heaven" refers to an entity, not a place. "Heaven" is used a lot in this context, and the concept has its roots in Taoism and Confucianism, two ancient religions in China. The emperor would worship and pay respect to heaven on an annual basis.

This phrase is often used to comfort people when an expected outcome is not realized. This tells the person that the negative result was not due to his or her shortcomings but was beyond the person's ability to control.

Chapter 7: Fortune Cookies

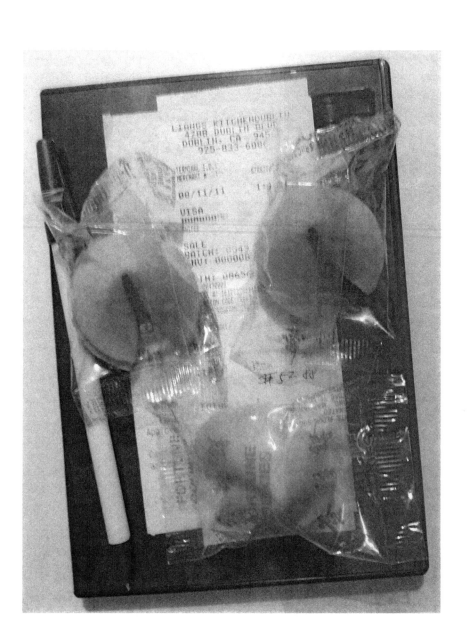

Fortune Cookies

At the end of most Chinese meals in Western countries, diners are given fortune cookies with various good-fortune sayings on paper inside them.

If you are looking for stories on fortune cookies in this book, you won't find them!

Fortune cookies originated in the United States and are usually offered to customers of Chinese restaurants at the end of a meal, usually with the check. They are not part of Chinese culture.

Hence, you will not find any cultural stories about fortune cookies in ancient China! Sorry!

Conclusion

Suggestions on Further Study

A culture with four thousand years of history cannot be properly covered in two hundred pages. With this book, I have tried to help individuals from the West to better understand their Chinese counterparts and to anticipate some of the key differences that they may experience from a cultural perspective.

For those with continuing interest, there are libraries full of wonder in all areas of human endeavor in China. But the key building blocks of Chinese culture to start with, on the road to growing one's understanding, are, of course, the writings by Confucius. Then there are a few classic standards that are important both for the perspective that they shed on Chinese culture and history and for their universal message. These include "Three Kingdoms" and *The Art of War*.

Another approach that I have found to be useful, educational, and fun is to look for Chinese children's books on proverbs and idioms. These books are typically simple stories and are written in simple English with illustrations. They are easy to understand and reflective of the continuing themes of Chinese culture.

For those with a true commitment, learning to speak Mandarin is the best way to begin developing a true and deep understanding of China and the culture of its people.

Last but not least, to understand the culture of a country, one needs to physically visit it. I know readers will enjoy visiting China after reading this book. Visiting a country allows you to appreciate the country and the people so much better, especially a country such as China, one of the oldest and deepest civilizations of the world.

Xie xie!   Thank you!

About the Authors

Born in China and brought up in Myanmar, Ed Yang graduated from National Taiwan University with a BSc and earned his MS from the University of Massachusetts and later his PK-E MBA from Pepperdine University. Ed started early in life on a long wonderful journey that has not ended. Ed's passion is people and the way they interact, get to know one another, and work together. For many American and Chinese individuals and companies, this has made Ed both a friend and a common source of advice and perspective on ways to bridge the divide that sometimes arises between cultures across the Pacific.

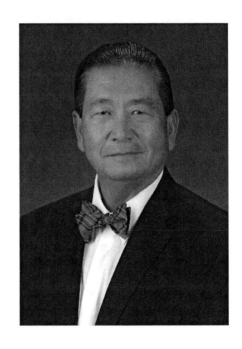

Beginning in the 1980s, constant travel between Asia and the United States in leadership positions with great companies such as EDS and Wang Laboratories gave Ed the ability to put his skills to work with great success, and he helped to create two of the largest technology businesses in Asia. Today, Ed is the chairman and president of iSoftStone Inc., the North American business unit of one of China's leading software services companies. He is also a frequent speaker at corporate and educational events on Chinese–American cross-cultural issues, including recent engagements with Microsoft, UBS, MIT Sloan School conferences, and Pepperdine University, where he has served on the Board of Regents for fifteen years. Most recently in July 2013, Ed was appointed the adjunct professor position with the Department of Management of the Business School of the Chinese University of Hong Kong.

Ultimately, Ed's passion is people—and helping people to understand people. Whether he is helping a 6'5" cowboy from Texas make sense out of Confucius or a petite Chinese woman comprehend a hard-charging American trying to make a point, Ed is someone who loves to help. And Ed often finds that the best way to make a point is with one of his favorite subjects—food! There is no message that cannot be conveyed with a good food analogy, or even better, a great meal!

When he is not on a plane or traveling in China or throughout the United States, Ed lives in Southern California and enjoys tennis, golf, swimming, and, more importantly, hanging around with his wife, his kids, his dog, his grandchildren, and of course a lobster!

Kate Ou is a technologist in software engineering. Born and educated in China, she graduated from Central South University in China and then received her MS in Japan at Kobe University. Kate has worked in a diverse range of tech companies, from start-ups in China and Japan to Microsoft in Redmond, Washington, where she has worked for thirteen years on a broad range of software development solutions and products.

Within the diverse organization of Microsoft, Kate has had the opportunity to work with talented individuals across many cultures and was actively involved as a board member from 2008 to 2010 of the Chinese Microsoft Employee Network (CHIME), a three-thousand-member community for which she organized and hosted various industry, career, and culture-related talks. She is the main author of the book *Microsoft 360 Success and Growth*.

Kate, who lives in Seattle, met Ed at a CHIME event and hosted Ed's talk in CHIME.

Dennis Smith's story is pretty much the opposite of Ed's. He was born and raised in Chicago and thought that he would be there pulling for the Cubs and the Bears his whole life. But somehow, the bank he worked for decided that he should be in Asia. That was in 1976. Thirty-seven years later, he's still there.

Dennis graduated from Loyola University of Chicago with a BA in 1973 and a MBA degree in 1975.

Since getting to Asia, Dennis has been a banker, a venture capitalist, a technologist, and a private equity investor across the region, but mostly in Greater China. He was fortunate to meet his "brother from another mother," Ed Yang, fifteen years ago.

Over the past four decades, quality of life has changed for the better for more people than at any time in the history of humankind. Dennis has witnessed that change and, like Ed, understands how important it is for people in China and the United States to understand what that means and why it is good for all if we work to understand one another.

Dennis is a partner with a large Hong Kong–based private equity firm and spends his time between Hong Kong and Hilton Head with his wife of thirty-plus years and his kids and grandkids.

Sby/.72

CPSIA information can be obtained at www.ICGtesting.com
Printed in the USA
BVOW07s0842041213

338023BV00006B/142/P